The Sponsor's 12 Step Manual:

Workbook Edition

A Guide to

Teaching and Learning the

Program of AA.

This is the Workbook Edition of The Sponsor's 12 Step Manual.

By John E

A
Get Into Recovery

The Sponsor's 12 Step Manual:
Workbook Edition.

ISBN-13: 978 - 1490485065
ISBN-10: 1490485066

First Edition June 2013.
Revised 2020

We are not affiliated with Alcoholics Anonymous
or any other 12 Step program.

Introduction.

This is not a stand-alone guide. For it to be successful you, must have access to the Big Book of Alcoholics Anonymous and The 12 Steps and 12 Traditions.

This Workbook Edition of The Sponsor's 12 Step Manual has additional space for writing answers.

An earlier version has been used with groups in treatment facilities in a classroom situation, and some people have set up home groups and met together using the earlier version as the basis for the meeting. The feedback has been very positive with people continuing to start other groups and the book being used as a tool to teach the Steps.

These groups have been lead by some experienced 12 Step facilitators who have given feedback on the use of the manual and some changes have occurred. Some comment has been made that the title "Analyzing" in the fourth level of each Step should not be used. That "Analyzing" can be an excuse for not taking action and one should always "utilize" what is in the Big Book and 12 Steps. This book is entirely about utilizing what is in the Big Book and 12 Steps and putting it into action.

The guide applies established educational techniques to developing an understanding of the 12 Steps of Alcoholics Anonymous. This process leads to a structure that progressively improves a person's knowledge and understanding of each of the steps examined. You will see when you start the book that it is broken down into different levels. There are 6 of these per Step, each one is progressively more challenging and asks you to take a different view of the Step you are looking at.

It is always recommended that the 12 Steps be worked with a sponsor. By the nature of the disease of addiction it is very easy to put your own interpretation on any of the materials presented to you.

Using Education theory to teach the 12 Steps.

Whilst on this journey of recovery I was fortunate enough to find myself on many training courses about education and came to believe that there are established educational theories that I could apply to teaching the 12 steps. I wrote my ideas down, so as to try to become a better sponsor, looking at each step in turn. I applied two of the theories to writing this book. The two pieces of work I studied are easy to digest and make sense to me. The first is written by William Glasser MD who states the following.

How We Learn
10% of what we READ
20% of what we HEAR
30% of what we SEE
50% of what we SEE and HEAR
70% of what is DISCUSSED with OTHERS
80% of what is EXPERIENCED PERSONALLY
95% of what we TEACH TO SOMEONE ELSE

The second piece of work was written by B S Bloom in 1956 and updated by Anderson, L W, & Krathwohl D R (eds.) in 2001. It states that we have different levels of learning and we should master one level before moving on to the next as follows.

Level 1 Remembering	Level 2 Understanding	Level 3 Applying
To recall something to mind.	Knowledge of a particular subject.	To make use of something to achieve a result.
Level 4 Analyzing	Level 5 Evaluating	Level 6 Creating
To examine something in great detail in order to understand it better.	To consider or examine something in order to judge its value, quality or importance.	Give rise to something or make something happen.

I looked at each of the 12 steps and applied these processes to that step in order to produce a progressive learning curve. It is suggested that not all of these categories be mastered by the sponsee before moving on to the next step.

That is to say that if a person is really struggling then the sponsor should make the decision to move on and revisit, rather than get stuck.

Step 1. "We admitted we were powerless over alcohol - that our lives had become unmanageable."

Remembering Step 1.

The first level of learning is to remember the subject, this is a vital stage in the learning process but may feel a bit pointless or autocratic. The benefits of learning each step so that it can be recalled from memory are tremendous in many ways, not only is it the foundation of further learning but remembering the steps 'off by heart' will lead to the reduction in feelings of isolation. You or your sponsee will feel more at home in a meeting. Ask him/her to learn Step 1 off by heart.

....

....

....

Understanding Step 1.

For the second level of learning, you must be able to explain the meaning and idea of Step 1. To begin the process of understanding this Step, you should take a look at some of the language used. Discuss the words written below and explain them in your own words.

*For this version of the Sponsor's Manual there are word definitions in the **back of the book**. Once you have written your own definition (or flick to the back if you want a quick peek) check with those written in the back of the book and compare your ideas.*

What is the meaning of the word **"admitted"** in Step 1?

....

....

There are many descriptions of being "**powerless**" Write down your own understanding before checking with the appendix.

....

....

....

The word "**unmanageable**" has various meanings. Write down what it means to you.

....

....

....

Next we shall put each definition into the context of Step 1.

"**admitted we were powerless over alcohol**."

Discuss being powerless over alcohol and what this means to you. Working together, explore general examples of powerlessness not related to alcohol. Concentrate on the concept of being powerless itself. Write down what powerless means to you, or make bullet points.

....

....

....

....

"that our lives had become unmanageable."

Describe areas of your own life that are, or have been, out of control. Which of these incidences are a result of alcohol? Which have been difficult or impossible to manage? Are there any times in your life that were unmanageable when you were not drinking? Make some notes below.

....

....

....

....

....

....

....

....

Applying Step 1.

Choose a time when you wanted to control your drinking; how successful were you? What went wrong? (i.e. promising to only have two drinks at a party). Make some notes below so you can discuss this with another.

....

....

....

....

....

....

....

Write about a time when you avoided people that were not drinking, or you hid your drinking from them.

....

....

....

....

....

....

....

....

Choose a period in your life that was unmanageable, e.g. missed appointments or constant lateness and write about it.

....

....

....

....

....

....

....

....

How has drinking affected your self-respect or self-image?

....

....

....

....

....

Discuss why the above questions are related to Step 1 and make some notes.

....

....

....

....

....

....

....

....

Analyzing Step 1. (Big Book and 12 and 12 Study Section)
Analyzing is the fourth level of learning. At this level, you will need to examine AA writings about powerlessness and unmanageability. This is a great learning opportunity, the work may seem arduous but the benefits are worth the effort.

To complete this section you will need to read Alcoholics Anonymous Chapter 3' "More About Alcoholism", "The Doctors Opinion" and then Step 1 in the 12 Steps and 12 Traditions.

In order to make the learning process easier during this section, a list of questions is added below. These will help focus you on specific points in each chapter. You will have to study each chapter to find the answers. They are not always obvious to find and not necessary in order. This section can take some effort.

Questions on "The Doctors Opinion."

1.What does the chapter say about the allergy?

....

....

....

2. What does the term' a psychic change' mean?

....

....

....

3. What effort is required to stay sober?

....

....

....

4. Why does Dr Silkworth believe that addiction is not entirely a problem of mental control?

....

....

....

5. What are the five types of alcoholic that the doctor classifies? Which ones do you identify with?

....

....

....

....

....

6. What is the 'only relief' suggested?

....

....

The next questions are focusing on Chapter 3, More About Alcoholism.

7. What illusion are we pursuing?

....

....

8. What delusion has to be smashed?

....

....

....

9. What have we lost?

....

....

....

10. What are you not going to believe, and why?

....

....

....

....

....

11. List the methods that have been tried in order to drink like other people.

....

....

....

....

....

....

....

12. How can you diagnose yourself?

....

....

....

....

13. What belief did 'The Man of Thirty' fall victim to?

....

....

....

14. What is particularly true of women?

....

....

....

15. What examples of Step 1 are highlighted by Jim's story?

....

....

....

....

....

16. How does the jaywalker story emphasise powerlessness?

....

....

....

....

17. Read Fred's story and write about what he realized when he regained his ability to think.

....

....

....

....

....

....

18. Why would Fred have to throw out several lifelong concepts?

....

....

....

19. Finish reading the chapter. What does it say we have no mental defence against?

....

....

....

I have often heard people tell of their inability to relate fully to the stories in this chapter during early recovery, only to revisit them at a later date and then, at that later date, really be able to absorb the meanings in full. Consider revisiting at a future date.

Questions on Step 1 in the 12 and 12

20. What does utter defeat enable us to do?

....

....

....

21. What is one of the facts of AA life?

....

....

....

22. Why is self-confidence no good whatsoever?

....

....

....

23. Why is alcohol a double-edged sword?

....

....

....

....

24. In A.A.'s pioneering time, only the most desperate people got well. In the following years this changed to include whom?
What were they spared?

....

....

....

....

....

25. What could we show them that changed their attitude?

....

....

....

26. Why all this insistence that every AA must hit a bottom first?

....

....

....

....

27. How low must your downfall be?

....

....

....

Evaluating with Step 1.
The fifth level of learning is evaluation. The task here is to evaluate ideas and learn to see outcomes that could have been different if you had not been drinking or drugging. Write some notes.

Select a time when you were angry towards someone whilst drinking. What may have been different if you were not drinking?Can you defend your behaviour, or can you support the idea that it would have been different if you were sober?

....

....

....

....

....

....

Compare the difference between stopping drinking and pausing drinking. An example of this could be - "Yeah, I stopped for 3 weeks once so I can't be an alcoholic". Forgot to add "then got drunk for a month" Write down your thoughts.

....

....

....

....

....

....

How does your personality change when you are under the influence of drink or drugs?

....

....

....

....

....

What things have you done to maintain your addiction that you said you would never do?

....

....

....

....

....

Have you ever been in real danger and been so 'out of it' you were completely vulnerable? Write a summary.

....

....

....

....

....

....

....

....

....

Complete this task: Work out the monetary cost of drinking. Produce a spreadsheet, graph or chart showing the amount of money spent over the drinking time; it does not have to be exact, just a rough estimate. How much could you have saved?

Comment has been made that cost is much more than just what has been spent on buying alcohol, there may have been other costs involved, describe some of these as well as completing your chart.

....

....

....

....

....

....

....

....

....

....

....

....

Creating with Step 1.
The sixth level of learning is the ability to apply what has been learned to creating something new. Here you should create some new discussion points that will highlight powerlessness and unmanageability that can be talked over with a newcomer, or in a group. This will help to increase your understanding as well as others. Write your ideas down below and discuss them with your sponsor or the person in authority before proceeding to take a group or meet newcomers.

....

....

....

Step 2. "Came to believe that a power greater than ourselves could restore us to sanity."

Remembering Step 2.
You should learn Step 2 off by heart. It is easy to skip this vital level but the benefits of learning the step verbatim are great. This will be the format from now on.

....

....

....

This will be the format from now on. Perhaps it could prompt you to learn all the steps off by heart.

Understanding Step 2.
You must be able to explain the meaning and idea of Step two.

To begin the process of understanding this Step take a look at some of the language used. Write a quick definition in your own words then flip to the back of the book to see the dictionary definitions. How do they compare?

"**Believe.**" What does believe mean? Write your own ideas.

....

....

....

....

What does the word **"power"** mean to you?

....

....

....

What is meant by the word **"greater"**?

....

....

....

Write about the meaning of being **"restored"**.

....

....

....

....

How would you describe **'sanity'**?

....

....

....

The next task is to put each definition into the context of Step 2.

"Came to believe." Discuss why is this written in the past tense? Write down your own understanding.

....

....

....

....

....

....

"A power greater than ourselves." What is a power greater than ourselves? Give your own understanding.

....

....

....

....

....

....

We often use higher powers but seldom think of them as that. Write down your own opinion on using higher powers.

....

....

....

....

....

....

....

....

"Restore us to sanity." Discuss the following then write down your ideas.

If you are behaving sanely then what would that look like to others? Write some short notes.

....

....

....

....

....

....

....

The next question I feel is important to place at this point. Explain the mental twist of alcoholism as described in the Big Book page 92.

....

....

....

....

....

....

Try to describe in your own words an understanding of sanity and insanity as applied to alcohol.

....

....

....

....

....

....

....

....

Applying Step 2.
You must be able to apply the information learned previously in this Step to personal experiences. From what you have learned already, write some short notes using the headings below.

Choose a time when your behavior may have been described by others as insane.

....

....

....

....

....

....

Give an example of a higher power helping in a situation that may have been unresolved unless help was obtained.

....

....

....

....

....

....

Write about a time in your life when you realized that you had to change. Did anyone help you?

....

....

....

....

....

....

Discuss how the above questions relate to this Step?

Analyzing Step 2. (Big Book and 12 and 12 Study Section)
At this level, you will need to examine AA writings about Step 2. To complete this section you will need to read Alcoholics

Anonymous Chapter 4 "We Agnostics", and Step 2 in the 12 Steps and 12 Traditions.

In order to make the learning process easier during this section, a list of questions has been added below. These will help focus you on specific points in each chapter. The next questions are focusing on Chapter 4 in the Big Book.

Chapter 4 "We Agnostics"

1. What are not always easy alternatives to face? Why?

....

....

....

2. What is our dilemma?

....

....

....

3. What exactly is this book about?

....

....

....

4. What difficulties arise with agnostics?

....

....

....

5. What is it we discover, much to our relief?

....

....

....

6. What is the one short question we need to ask ourselves?

....

....

....

7. What are the 'good reasons' to believe in a power greater than ourselves?

....

....

....

8. On page 52, what should we apply to our human problem? What subjects does the Big Book give as examples?

....

....

....

....

....

....

9. What 'certain kind' of faith does the Big Book say we already have?

....

....

....

10. What idea is deep down in every man, woman and child?

....

....

....

11. In the story of the atheist, what was the turning point in this mans recovery?

....

....

....

The following are based on Step 2, in the 12 and 12:

12. This chapter identifies five different cases of religious belief, or disbelief, what are they?

....

....

....

....

....

13. How does a sponsor respond to someone who says he won't believe?

....

....

....

....

14. What are the three statements?

....

....

....

....

....

....

15. What can we say to someone who has lost faith?

....

....

....

16. What does the intellect have to do to become right sized?

....

....

....

17. Those who are 'disgusted with religion' have substituted negative for positive thinking. What do they have to realize?

....

....

....

18. What is the outstanding characteristic of many an alcoholic?

....

....

....

19. A man full of faith needs to do what?

....

....

....

20. As an example of "surrender to win", what suggestion may not be endured?

....

....

Evaluating with Step 2.

Here you are looking to identify times in your own life that could be considered insane. Some questions to answer could be:

Select a time when your behavior was insane or even just illogical. Were there any times that someone or something intervened to alter the outcome? Can you support the idea that, without this higher power, the consequences would have been a lot worse?

....

....

....

....

....

....

....

....

Defend the idea that we cannot restore our sanity on our own and need a higher power in our lives to guide and nurture us back to right thinking.

....

....

....

....

....

....

....

....

What have your previous experiences been with religion? Consider whether this does or does not change your belief of God as you understand Him?

....

....

....

....

....

....

What changes in your *thinking* are necessary to restore you to sanity?

....

....

....

....

....

....

....

....

....

What changes in your *behavior* are necessary to restore you to sanity?

....

....

....

....

....

....

....

....

....

Creating with Step 2.

Here you are to create a list of discussion points that may be discussed with a newcomer, or in a group, that will highlight a power greater than ourselves and how that power can restore us to sanity. This is as important for you as it is for the newcomer. Discuss with your sponsor before proceeding.

....

....

....

....

....

....

....

....

....

....

....

....

....

....

Step 3. "Made a decision to turn our will and our lives over to the care of God as we understood Him."

Remembering Step 3.
Again focusing on that very important level of 'Remembering' learn Step 3 so that you are able to recite it by heart.

....

....

....

Understanding Step 3.
To begin the process of understanding this Step take a look at some of the language used. Write a definition in your own words then flip to the back of the book to see the dictionary definitions, how do they compare?

What is a **"decision"**?

....

....

....

In this context, **'our will'** means our 'self-will'. What does self will mean to you?

....

....

....

In the phrase 'our will and our lives', what does the word **'lives'** mean in this context?

....

....

....

What does **'care'** mean?

....

....

....

How do you explain "**God**?" **Phew!**

....

....

....

What is the meaning of "**understood**"?

....

....

....

Next we shall put each definition into the context of the Step.

"Made a decision".

Discuss what it means to make a decision.

Talk about any decision made that, if not followed by action is still only a decision. Here I would like to insert the story I heard about frogs. (Heard in an AA meeting)

Three frogs are sitting on a log when two decide to jump off into the water. Question: How many frogs are left on the log?

Answer, three. They only made a decision. Write a few notes on your understanding of this.

....

....

....

....

....

....

"our will and our lives"

Discuss what it means by "our will and our lives"

Another discussion point could be: Why our will **AND** our lives?

Self-will, as defined in the Oxford English Dictionary, is given as "Obstinately doing what one wants in spite of the wishes or orders of others'. Discuss the point that we were running our lives obstinately making decisions based on our own will rather than using the wisdom of others. Write a few notes.

....

....

....

....

....

....

....

....

"God as we understood Him"

Discuss your understanding of God. Remember that this is your own conception not anyone else's. Write your ideas down.

....

....

....

....

....

Applying Step 3.

Your must be able to apply the information learned previously in this Step to personal experiences. From what you have learned already write some notes demonstrating the ideas and concepts of step 3. Use the headings below.

Describe in writing or draw a picture of God as you understand Him.

....

....

....

....

....

....

....

Write down the characteristics or behaviors of someone running on self-will. Then do the same for someone who has made a decision to run their life according to the will of a beneficial higher power.

Self Will

....

....

....

....

Higher Power

....

....

....

....

When making a decision about something, describe in writing the process that you should follow, especially in early recovery.

....

....

....

....

....

....

....

....

....

Discuss how the above questions relate to this Step?

Analyzing Step 3. (Big Book and 12 and 12 Study Section)
At this level, you will need to examine AA writings about Step 3. To complete this section you should read Alcoholics Anonymous Chapter 5, "How it Works" up to the bottom of page 63 and Step 3 in the 12 and 12. Some questions are added below to guide your teaching. Write some short answers.

These questions focus on **"How it Works."**

1. Many people do recover, if they have what?

....

....

....

2. Why do you need to let go of your old ideas?

....

....

....

3. How does this chapter describe alcohol? (This could also be addiction.)

....

....

....

4. What do half measures achieve? Why?

....

....

5. What are the 'Steps we took?' (Write them out it will help you learn them)

....

....

....

....

6. What are the three pertinent ideas?

....

....

....

....

....

....

7. What is the first requirement?

....

....

....

8. What are most of us concerned with?

....

....

....

....

9. If our troubles are of our own making, where do they arise from?

....

....

....

10. What do we need to quit playing?

....

....

11. Whom should you take this Step with?

....

....

12. What should we do next?

....

....

....

....

....

The next questions focus on **Step 3**, in the 12 and 12.

13. What is the only key we need?

....

14. What does Step 3 call for?

....

....

....

15. What have we done without realizing it?

....

....

16. Dependence on a higher power seems weak, but what do the facts seem to be?

....

....

....

....

17. Once our independence is in question, how do we behave?

....

....

....

....

18. What might you do if the image in the mirror is too awful?

....

....

....

19. Why can we alcoholics consider ourselves fortunate?

....

....

....

20. List some wrong forms of dependence. i.e parents for money.

....

....

....

....

....

....

....

21. How did A.As cope when World War II broke out?

....

....

....

22. How can a willing person continue to turn his will and his life over?

....

....

....

23. Often people are convinced that they should have no self-will at all. This is not true. How is this explained in the paragraph beginning "Then it is explained" (page 41). Write a brief summary.

....

....

....

....

....

....

....

....

....

24. So what had our whole trouble been?

....

....

....

....

....

Evaluating with Step 3.

The task here is to evaluate ideas or importance and learn to see outcomes that could have been different, if you had not

been drinking or drugging. Some questions to answer could
be:

Select a time when you have made a decision on your own
that turned out to be the wrong one. What may have been
different if you had listened to others?

....

....

....

....

....

....

....

....

....

....

....

....

Did you make a decision and still carry it out even though you knew it was wrong?

Did your pride or anger not allow you to back down?

Write a summary.

....

....

....

....

....

....

....

....

....

....

....

....

Creating with Step 3.

Here you are to create a list of discussion points that may be discussed with a newcomer, or in a group, that will highlight the problems of running a life on self-will. There may be other points that you think you could cover on this Step that will be helpful to others. Make note of them all. Discuss with another before leading a group or talking to a newcomer.

....

....

....

....

....

....

....

....

....

....

....

....

Step 4. "Made a searching and fearless moral inventory of ourselves."

Remembering Step 4.
Here we are again, another step to commit to memory. If you find this a bit repetitive that's because it is. Remind your yourself or your group that this is the first level of learning and forms the bedrock on which all else is built.

....

....

....

Understanding Step 4.
Your must be able to explain the meaning and idea of Step 4.

To begin the process of understanding this Step take a look at some of the language used. Write a quick definition in your own words then flip to the back of the book to see the dictionary definitions, how do they compare?

What does "**searching**" mean?

....

....

....

How do you define "**fearless**"?

....

....

Your explanations of the word "**moral**" is:

....

....

....

What is an "**inventory**"?

....

....

....

Next put each definition into the context of the Step.

Made a "**searching and fearless**".

Discuss what it means to make 'a searching and fearless inventory' of someone's life? Write down some of your ideas.

....

....

....

....

....

....

"moral inventory."

Discuss what a moral inventory is? We know what these words mean individually but what do they mean when combined? Make some notes.

....

....

....

....

....

....

Applying Step 4.

You must be able to apply the information learned previously in this Step to personal experiences. From what you have learned already write some notes on your understanding of Step 4 so far. Here are some headings that may prompt you.

Give a description of how you could construct a moral inventory. (Not what's in it).

....

....

....

....

....

Examine how you feel about this step. Does completing a fearless search of yourself give rise to a sense of anxiety, excitement or freedom?

....

....

....

....

....

....

Do you blame others and make excuses for your own behavior? Write about some times when you have.

....

....

....

....

....

....

....

....

Give an example of your own dishonesty in regards to
manipulating or lying to a loved one.

....

....

....

....

....

....

....

Discuss how the above questions related to Step 4?

Analyzing Step 4. (Big Book and 12 and 12 Study Section)
At this level, you will need to examine AA's writings about
taking a moral inventory.

To complete this section you will need to read Alcoholics Anonymous Chapter 5 "How it Works" from the bottom of page 63 to the end of the chapter, and Step 4 in the 12 and 12.

Some questions are written below to help direct you towards key points. Write your answers.

The first questions are based on **Chapter 5**.

1. What vigorous course of action should we take and why?

....

....

....

....

....

2. So what is Step 4?

....

....

....

3. What does this chapter compare a personal inventory to?

....

....

....

4. Why are we searching out the flaws in our make up?

....

....

....

5. What is the number one offender? Why?

....

....

....

....

6. What should be included in our grudge list?

....

....

....

7. What business is infinitely grave?

....

....

....

8. Why is anger a poison to us?

....

....

....

9. How should we react if someone offends us?

....

....

....

10. Why should we put out of our minds the wrongs others had done?

....

....

....

11. What does this chapter say about fear?

....

....

....

12. Read the paragraph on sex. How should we treat this subject?

....

....

....

13. When reviewing your own conduct, what should you be looking for?

....

....

....

14. Why should you avoid hysterical thinking or advice?

....

....

....

15. What should you do if sex is very troublesome?

....

....

....

16. If you have been thorough about your personal inventory what will you have achieved?

....

....

....

The next questions focus on Step 4 in the 12 and 12.

17. What do our instincts often far exceed? Give examples.

....

....

....

....

....

....

....

....

18. What is Step 4 trying to discover?

....

....

....

19. If a person is on the depressive side, what is likely to happen when you probe their instincts?

....

....

....

20. What is likely to happen when you investigate someone's instincts who is self righteous or grandiose?

....

....

....

21. What is another excuse for avoiding an inventory?

....

....

....

22. How can a sponsor come to the rescue of these three persons?

....

....

....

....

....

....

....

....

23. What are our more glaring personality defects?

....

....

....

....

....

24. What conclusion will the newcomer have arrived at?

....

....

....

....

....

....

25. How can a person start a personal inventory? What questions are apt? Write them down.

....

....

....

....

....

....

Evaluating with Step 4.

The task here is to evaluate ideas or importance. Some questions for you may be:

Do you think there is a better way to clear out the wreckage of the past and perform a personal housecleaning?

....

....

....

Demonstrate, verbally or in writing, why we should do a moral inventory. Why is it so important?

....

....

....

Examine the Big Books templates for creating an inventory. Why do you think they are laid out in this way? Why do you think people may have re-designed them?

....

....

....

....

....

....

Evaluate some of your own qualities. Which ones do you like, which ones do others like?

....

....

....

....

....

....

Creating with Step 4.
Here you have to create a Step 4 inventory. Use the same format as in the Big Book unless you have decided on a template you prefer. Complete this on paper or a template that you can keep separate. You may not wish others to see your inventory.

You are also to create a list of discussion points to help increase the understanding of Step 4 for newcomers or your group. This should include the key points of this Step. Talk them over with another before proceeding to run a group or speak to someone new.

....

....

....

....

....

....

....

....

....

....

....

....

Step 5. "Admitted to God, to ourselves, and to another human being the exact nature of our wrongs."

Remembering Step 5.
This first stage of learning Step 5 by heart is a must. It is tempting to skip this level; however, you must be able to recall Step 5 and recite it back to yourself. Start by writing it down.

....

....

....

....

Understanding Step 5.
To begin the process of understanding this Step take a look at some of the language used. Write a quick definition in your own words then flip to the back of the book to see the dictionary definitions, how do they compare?

What does the word "**admitted**" mean?

....

....

....

How "**exact**" is exact? What does it mean?

....

....

The word "**nature**" has many meanings. What does it mean in this context?

....

....

....

What do you understand by the word "**wrongs**"?

....

....

....

Next we shall put the words that you have defined into the context of the Step.

"**admitted to**"

Discuss what it means to admit to something. Are we just admitting? i.e. 'Yeah I did that' or are we making an acknowledgment of past mistakes to make a clean start? Write a note or two.

....

....

....

....

....

"God, ourselves, and another human being".

There are important reasons for admitting to the above three things,. Discuss with your peers why you think all three are included and write some notes.

....

....

....

....

....

....

....

"the exact nature of our wrongs".

Explain what we mean by "exact nature". What wrongs are we focussing on? This looks like a small question but the answer can be substantial. Write down your thoughts.

....

....

....

....

....

....

....

....

....

Applying Step 5.

You must be able to apply the information learned previously in this Step to personal experiences. Write a short paragraph using the questions below, including why they relate to Step 5.

Write a short piece on why we need the feedback of another person. Do we have the ability to see all the missing pieces of the jigsaw puzzle on our own?

....

....

....

....

....

....

....

....

....

....

From what you know of Step 5 write a list of the sort of things we are admitting to, i.e. **types** of behavior rather than specific incidences. (Jealousy etc)

....

....

....

....

....

....

Debate, in writing, the need to complete a stock taking and house cleaning exercise.

....

....

....

....

....

....

....

....

....

Analyzing Step 5. (Big Book and 12 and 12 Study Section)
At this level you will need to examine AA's writings about Step 5 and compare them to your own ideas.

To complete this section you will need to read Alcoholics Anonymous Chapter 6, "Into Action" and Step 6 in the 12 and 12. In order to make the learning process easier a list of questions has again been included to help you focus on certain points within the Step.

The below questions focus on Chapter 6.

1. What is it we are trying to get and discover?

....

....

....

2. What may people find difficult?

....

....

....

3. What is the 'best reason' for not skipping this Step?

....

....

....

4. Why does this chapter compare the alcoholic to an actor?

....

....

....

....

5. What have we seldom told psychologists (or others)? What has this lead to?

....

....

....

....

....

....

6. What must we be if we want to live long and happily?

....

....

....

7. What guidance does this chapter give to finding the person whom we will share our 5th Step with?

....

....

....

....

....

....

8. What have we no right to do?

....

....

....

9. Why might we postpone this Step? What are the dangers of this?

....

....

....

....

....

10. What should your chosen partner realize?

....

....

....

11. What should you withhold when you take this Step?

....

12. After sharing this Step, what does the program recommend you do?

....

....

....

....

....

These next questions are on Step 5 in the 12 Steps and 12 Traditions.

13. Why are few steps harder than Step 5?

....

....

....

14. Why may people try to bypass Step 5?

....

....

....

15. What has A.A.'s experience taught us about this?

....

....

....

....

16. Are religions the only advocates of admitting one's defects? Explain you answer.

....

....

....

....

....

17. What are we likely to receive from Step 5?

....

....

....

....

....

....

18. What key feelings about forgiveness do we find?

....

....

....

....

....

....

19. What other great dividend may we expect?

....

....

....

20. Why won't a solitary self-appraisal be enough?

....

....

....

....

....

....

21. What are the two difficulties of dealing with God ourselves?

....

....

....

....

....

22. Why is going it alone in spiritual matters dangerous?

....

....

....

23. What is our next problem?

....

....

24. What are the real tests of whom you share your self survey with?

....

....

....

....

25. What great moment is apt to occur?

....

....

....

Evaluating with Step 5.
This level is relatively easy for Step 5 and follows the Big Book to the word. Half way down page 75, starting 'Returning home' are the instructions on how to evaluate what we have

done so far. Follow these instructions after you have shared your inventory.

Sharing your inventory.

This is the time to share your 4th Step inventory. Remember the guidance that is written in the Big Book about whom you share it with.

Creating with Step 5.
The next task for you is to create a list of topic points that may be discussed with newcomers highlighting the key points of Step 5. Think about the process you took to learn the Steps and see if you can help others learn this Step in a similar way. Talk this over with your sponsor before proceeding to talk to new comers.

....

....

....

....

....

....

....

Step 6. "Were entirely ready to have God remove all these defects of character."

Remembering Step 6.
You must be able to quote Step 6 from memory before moving on to the next level. To start help this process write it down.

....

....

....

....

Understanding Step 6.
To begin the process of understanding this Step take a look at some of the language used. Write a quick definition in your own words then flip to the back of the book to see the dictionary definitions, how do they compare?

What does **"entirely"** mean?

....

....

....

What does **"remove"** mean?

....

....

Some definitions of **"defects"** are;

....

....

....

What does "**character**" mean in this Step?

....

....

....

Try and define the two meanings below in your own words.

"Were entirely ready to have God remove".

....

....

....

"Defects of character".

....

....

....

How do you start to recognize your own defects of character? A list is written at the end of this book to help you think about this. The left side of the list is the shortcoming and the right side its opposite.

Applying Step 6.
You must be able to apply the information learned previously in this Step to personal experiences. From what you have learned already, write a short paragraph on defects of character and removing them.

....

....

....

....

....

....

....

....

Describe situations and events where you have been dishonest. What problems has it caused you? What would have been an honest way to have handled the situation?

....

....

....

....

....

Describe situations and events where you have been angry. What problems has it caused you? What would have been a calm way to have handled the situation?

....

....

....

....

....

....

....

....

Describe situations and events where you have been jealous. What problems has it caused you? What would have been a trusting way to have handled the situation?

....

....

....

....

....

....

....

Discuss why these questions applicable to Step 6?

Analyzing Step 6. (Big Book and 12 and 12 Study Section)
At this level, you will need to examine AA's writings about step 6 and compare them to your own ideas.

Starting at page 76 in Alcoholics Anonymous, ending with the Step 7 prayer two paragraphs later, read this part of Chapter 6 "Into Action". To cover this step in greater depth read Step 6 in the 12 Steps and 12 Traditions, these questions will help direct you to significant points.

Answer these questions on Step 6 in the 12 and 12.

1. Why is this Step the one that separates the men from the boys?

....

....

....

2. What statements are heard daily all over the world?

....

....

....

3. What is it every normal person wants?

....

....

....

4. What happens when we let our natural desires drive us?

....

....

....

5. What are we supposed to be working towards?

....

....

....

6. What do we need to have patient improvement in?

....

....

7. What is the "best we can do"?

....

....

....

8. If you have escaped the extremes of glaring handicaps, can you congratulate yourself?

....

....

....

....

9. Why can self-righteous anger be enjoyable?

....

....

....

10. What is it we prefer to hang on to?

....

....

....

11. Which is the only Step that can be practiced with absolute perfection.

....

....

....

12. What should the only question be?

....

....

....

13. So what does that make the other 11 Steps?

....

....

14. What should we not say to ourselves?

....

....

....

15. Summarize the end of this chapter starting with what happens the moment we say "no never".

....

....

....

....

....

Evaluating with Step 6.
You are to consider and examine your own defects of character, which you will write down in the next section. A list of personality traits and their opposites are given at the end of the book for you to consider. Take a look at this and use it as a basis for exploring your own defects. In the list is included the

opposite of the negative trait so as to give pause for thought on what it is you could work on to balance out your own defects.

Some people have commented that this has left them feeling very negative about themselves. If you wish, construct a list of all the positive things about yourself, this can be very difficult and you may need the help of another.

Creating with Step 6.
You are to create a list of your own character defects in preparation for Step 7. Don't be over critical.

....

....

....

....

....

....

....

....

....

Also create a list of discussion points that can be talked over with a newcomer, or in your group, that will highlight character defects, having them removed and being ready to have them removed.

....

....

....

....

....

....

....

....

....

....

....

....

....

Step 7. "Humbly asked Him to remove our shortcomings."

Remembering Step 7.
The first task on every Step is to learn it parrot fashion. There may not be many words to this step but there is a lot to work on. Start by writing it down.

....

....

....

Understanding Step 7.
You must be able to explain the meaning and idea of Step 7.

To begin the process of understanding this Step take a look at some of the language used. Write a quick definition in your own words then flip to the back of the book to see the dictionary definitions, how do they compare?

Explore what the word **"humbly"** means. Does it mean to be subservient and less than? Could it mean the opposite of arrogant? Write some of your ideas down.

....

....

....

....

....

Your definitions of "**shortcomings**" are;

....

....

....

....

....

Putting those words together in Step 7 we get -

"**Humbly** asked Him."

Discuss this sentence - "Am I trying to be modest in my request knowing that I want and need help from others"? Write down your opinion of this statement.

....

....

....

"**Remove** our shortcomings."

Write down your ideas on what is meant by the word "**remove**". Is this permanent or do we need to continue to work on these issues?

....

....

....

Are shortcomings and character defects the same?

....

Applying Step 7.
You must be able to apply the information learned previously in this Step to personal experiences. From what you have learned already write a short response to the headings below.

Describe in writing what you think that your life will be like with your defects of character removed from you.

....

....

....

....

....

....

....

....

What defects will be most difficult to give up? Write down why you will find these most difficult.

....

....

....

....

....

....

....

....

What kind of situations or pressure could cause you to regress back into your defects of character? What can you do about it? Summarize your thoughts in a paragraph.

....

....

....

....

....

....

....

....

Discuss how these questions relate to Step 7.

Analyzing Step 7. (Big Book and 12 and 12 Study Section)
Again there is little in the Big Book on Step 7; so to cover this in greater depth read Step 7 in the 12 Steps and 12 Traditions. Some questions are written below to highlight key points.

1. What does Step 7 concern itself with?

....

....

....

2. What is our crippling handicap?

....

....

....

3. What have we never thought of making our daily basis of living?

....

....

....

4. What makes a working faith in a higher power impossible?

....

....

....

5. What can be unbelievably painful?

....

....

....

....

6. What first milestone do we learn?

....

....

....

7. What inescapable conclusion drives us?

....

....

....

8. What happens after we have taken a square look at some of these defects?

....

....

....

9. What changes in our outlook does this improved perception start?

....

....

....

....

....

....

....

10. What had been the admission price of a new life?

....

....

....

11. What profound change is the result of learning?

....

....

12. What might our deeper objectives be?

....

....

....

13. What is the chief activator of our defects?

....

....

....

14. So what is Step 7 really saying to us?

....

....

....

Evaluating with Step 7.
You are to make an evaluation of your Steps 6 and 7 and decide whether you have been honest about your defects. Have you kept hold of any that you are fond of or any that you are unwilling to let go of?

Creating with Step 7.
Your next task is to create the right time and environment to complete this phase of Step 7. This is where you will be reading the Step 7 prayer on page 76 in a fashion that best suits your personal preferences.

You are also to create a list of discussion points that can be talked about with a newcomer, or in a group, that will highlight Step 7. Remember to discuss what it is to be humble as many people misunderstand this word. Take these points to your sponsor before facilitating a session.

....

....

....

....

Step 8. "Made a list of all persons we had harmed, and became willing to make amends to them all."

Remembering Step 8.
Learn Step 8 from memory before moving on to the next level. To make a start, write it down.

....

....

....

....

....

Understanding Step 8.
You must be able to explain the meaning and idea of Step 8.

To begin the process of understanding this Step take a look at some of the language used. Write a quick definition in your own words then flip to the back of the book to see the dictionary definitions, how do they compare?

What is meant by "list"?

....

....

....

What do we mean by "**harmed**".

....

....

....

What is the meaning of "**willing**"?

....

....

....

Your definition of "**amends**" could be;

....

....

....

Next we shall put each definition in the context of the Step.

"Made a **list** of **all** persons we had **harmed**"

You can see from the first part of this step that when put these words are put together, the task is a lot harder than perhaps originally perceived. There is a lot more to think about than just the words. Discuss what the first part of the Step means and describe it in your own words.

....

....

....

....

....

....

Explain what is meant by "**all**" persons we had harmed?

....

....

....

"Became **willing** to make **amends** to them all".

Discuss this statement -

The word "**became**" is used because everyone who has attempted this Step was unwilling at first to be entirely ready to make that full commitment. Make some notes on what you talked about.

....

....

....

....

....

....

What is the main idea behind using the word **"All"** twice in this Step?

....

....

Applying Step 8.
You must be able to apply the information learned previously in this Step to personal experiences.

Some topics to write about could be:

What consequences do you fear in making amends?

....

....

....

....

....

....

....

....

What is the worst thing that can happen when making amends?

....

....

....

....

....

....

....

What is the best thing that can happen when making amends?

....

....

....

....

....

....

....

....

What is likely to happen when making amends?

....

....

....

....

....

....

....

....

....

....

Think of some of the people you have harmed and list the effect on them as individuals and on your relationship with them.

....

....

....

....

....

....

....

Describe any ways that you can use to get rid of the anger and resentment towards anyone on your list.

....

....

....

....

....

....

Discuss why these questions highlight Step 8?

Analyzing Step 8. (Big Book and 12 and 12 Study Section)
At this level, you will need to examine AA's writings about Step 8 and compare them to your own ideas. To complete this section you will need to read from Alcoholics Anonymous the middle of page 76, 'Now we need more action' to 'this thought' on page 84. There also follows questions on Step 8 in the 12 and 12.

The following questions will give you areas to focus on.

1. What do we need now?

....

....

....

2. What are we trying to repair?

....

....

....

3. On our first approach, what need we not do to some people?

....

....

....

....

....

4. What should we not do under any condition?

....

....

....

5. What happens in nine cases out of ten?

....

....

....

6. There are some general principles we should follow scattered over the next few pages. What are they?

....

....

....

....

....

....

....

....

....

....

....

7. What may you both decide is the way of good sense and loving kindness?

....

....

....

8. Why is the alcoholic like a tornado?

....

....

....

I think it also wise to read the story "Freedom from Bondage", in particular the part starting with 'If you have a resentment you want to be free of'. This is only a suggestion that may help some members. It is in the stories section so is not part of the instructions included in the first 164 pages. It does have merit and has worked for many.

The following questions are directed towards Step 8 in the 12 and 12.

9. What are Steps 8 and 9 concerned with?

....

....

10. What is a very large order?

....

....

....

11. There are a least four obstacles to Step 8. What are they?

....

....

....

....

....

....

....

12. As well as making restitution what else is equally necessary?

....

....

....

13. What might we next ask ourselves?

....

....

....

14. What subtler harms may we have committed?

....

....

....

15. What can we now commence to do?

....

....

....

16. What should we avoid?

....

....

....

17. What should this step be the beginning of the end of?

....

....

....

Evaluating with Step 8.

At this point you should re-examine your Step Four inventory for here will be a list of people that will populate your Step 8 list. Some people may have destroyed or burned their inventory in some sort of healing ritual and some may have destroyed it in case others find it. Not to worry if you have, you will find your memory is a lot sharper than it has been for a long time and it won't take much to populate a list again. You may also find that people needed to be added that weren't in your Step 4. This isn't to say that you didn't do a thorough Step 4, just that recovery is progressive and you may remember situations differently now from when you did your inventory.

Creating with Step 8.
There are now some areas to work on with the list. Study the list of people harmed, and form a plan of possible amends for each one of them. Always check your thinking with someone else, make sure that you don't rush headlong into amends that could harm yourself or others.

Your may wish to prioritize your list from easy amends to hard ones. Remember that in the Big Book it says that practice will make a person better at making amends, so start with the easy ones.

Don't *start making amends until you have completed the work on Step 9.*

You are also to create a list of discussion points that you can talk about with others that will highlight making amends and becoming willing. Talk these over with another before leading a discussion.

....

....

....

Step 9. "Made direct amends to such people wherever possible, except when to do so would injure them or others."

Remembering Step 9.
You must be able to recall Step 9 and recite it back to others from memory. Write it down to start the process of remembering.

....

....

....

....

....

....

Understanding Step 9.
To begin the process of understanding this Step take a look at some of the language used. Write a quick definition in your own words then flip to the back of the book to see the dictionary definitions, how do they compare?

What is meant by "**direct**"?

....

....

....

You have covered the meaning of "**amends**" in the previous Step but repetition is a key to learning. So what does it mean?

....

....

....

"**except when**" Most people will have no difficulty defining these words, however, because of its importance in this Step it is worthy of attention. What does this mean to you?

....

....

....

Again, a repetition but not time wasted. What do we mean by '**harmed**'?

....

....

....

Write below a meaning for the word '**injure**'.

....

....

....

Lets put those definitions together in the context of Step 9

Made "**direct amends**"

Discussion point: Why should you make direct amends rather than indirect amends? Is this strictly true?

Read the next sentence, then look at the question that follows.

"**except when** to do so would **injure** them"

Explore the idea that we could "injure them".
What sort of injuries could we cause?

....

....

....

"**Or others**" Discuss who those others might be. Make some notes.

....

....

....

....

....

....

....

Before making any amend, it is essential that they are discussed with a sponsor first.

Applying Step 9.
You must be able to apply the information learned previously in this step to personal experiences. Some headings to help could be:

What amends do you think that you have already made? How have you made them?

....

....

....

....

....

....

Write a short passage on why you should **not** make amends in certain circumstances and discuss this with another.

....

....

....

....

....

....

....

....

....

Take part in some role play with your sponsor or group and practice what you are going to say when making amends. (Rehearsal can be essential for some people; perhaps your partner could play devils advocate or be fantastically over friendly).

Analyzing Step 9. (Big Book and 12 and 12 Study Section)
At this level you will need to examine A.A.s writings about Step 9 and what it means to make direct amends.
These question focus on the latter part of "Into Action" from the Big Book Alcoholics Anonymous.

1. What must we take the lead in?

....

....

....

2. To whom should we not talk to incessantly and why?

....

....

....

....

....

....

3. What can we do if there are some wrongs we can never fully right?

....

....

....

....

....

4. What are we going to be if we are painstaking about this phase of our development? (First line only)

....

....

5. What is this paragraph otherwise known as in A.A.

....

....

The next questions focus on Step 9 in the 12 Steps and 12 Traditions.

6. What qualities shall we need when we take Step 9?

....

....

....

7. There are four classes can we divide our amends into, what are they?

....

....

....

....

....

....

....

....

8. When has the process of making amends begun?

....

....

....

9. Why do we only make a general admission of our defects at our first meeting with a family member?

....

....

....

....

....

10. What approach should we take at our place of work?

....

....

....

11. What reactions are likely to put us off balance?

....

....

....

12. What great temptation may you face?

....

....

....

13. What is it usually safe to do once you feel confident enough?

....

....

....

14. What one consideration should qualify our desire for complete disclosure?

....

....

....

15. What other razor edged questions may arise in other departments of life?

....

....

....

....

....

....

....

16. Why should we be absolutely sure we are not delaying?

....

....

....

Evaluating with Step 9.
At this point you should sit down with your sponsor, or counsellor, and ask him/her to evaluate your list of amends. Ask him/her to consider the list to see if it is achievable, over ambitious or whether you have shied away from some areas.

It is now the task of the sponsor to make a judgement as to whether certain amends should be made or not. Will it harm or heal? Is the timing right?

Making amends
Start on the amends and remember that you needs to do this with the support of a sponsor or counsellor.

Creating with Step 9.
Make a list of points that you can lead a group, or talk to a newcomer about, that covers the important parts of Step 9. Confirm you are on the right lines with another before running a group or speaking to a newcomer.

....

....

....

....

Step 10. "Continued to take personal inventory and when we were wrong promptly admitted it."

Remembering Step 10.
You must be able to recall Step 10 and be able to quote it if asked. Again start the process of by writing it down.

....

....

....

....

....

Understanding Step 10.
To begin the process of understanding this Step take a look at some of the language used. Write a quick definition in your own words then flip to the back of the book to see the dictionary definitions, how do they compare?

What does "**continued**" mean to you:

....

....

....

Write your definition of "**personal**":

....

....

"**inventory**". This word has been covered before, what is your understanding of it now?

....

....

....

....

....

What is your understanding of the word "**wrong**"?

....

....

....

The word "**promptly**" can be defined as below.

....

....

....

"admitted" Covered already but important nonetheless important.

....

....

Next, we shall put each definition into the context of Step 10.

"Continued to take personal inventory."

You know the meaning of **personal** and **inventory** as individual words. Write down your ideas of what they mean together.

....

....

....

....

....

....

Discuss with another what it means to take a personal inventory that is continuous. Jot down some notes.

....

....

....

....

....

....

"And when we were wrong"

Have a talk about knowing when you are wrong. Discuss with another person whether it is possible to spot your own wrong doings all of the time, some of the time or none of the time. Make a few notes.

....

....

....

....

....

....

....

....

....

Talk with another about the following statement. "It can be worthwhile setting up a system whereby you check with another person the wisdom of your actions before running headlong into a disastrous amend". Make some notes on what that system could be.

....

....

....

....

....

....

....

....

....

"Promptly admitted it"

How prompt do you need to be. Timing can be important. A question to answer could be "should I do this straight away?" Write down your thoughts.

....

....

....

....

....

....

Applying Step 10.

You must be able to apply the information learned previously in this Step to personal goals.

Construct a plan to allow time for reflection each day? Write it here.

....

....

....

....

....

....

....

....

....

....

....

....

Make a list of behaviors or attitudes that you will need to guard against in daily living.

....

....

....

....

....

....

....

....

....

Write a set of self-help instructions that you can follow if you find yourself in a position that puts you under pressure or you find hard to handle.

....

....

....

....

....

....

....

....

....

If not already working this Step, prompt yourself to start.

Analyzing Step 10. (Big Book and 12 and 12 Study Section)
At this level, you will need to examine AA writings about Step 10. To complete this section, you will need to continue to read "Into Action" starting on page 84 ("This thought brings us to step Ten"). Also read Step 10 in the 12 and 12.

These first questions focus on "Into Action", page 84.

1. What is the Step 10 suggestion?

....

....

....

....

2. So what should our next function be?

....

....

....

3. What is our code?

....

....

4. What have we ceased fighting?

....

5. Why are we neither cocky nor afraid?

....

....

....

....

....

....

....

....

6. What is our daily reprieve contingent on?

....

....

....

....

....

The following questions will help you study Step 10 in the 12 Steps and 12 Traditions:

7. What is the acid test?

....

....

....

8. What are necessities for us?

....

....

....

....

9. What other kind of hangover is there? How do you deal with it?

....

....

....

....

....

....

....

10. Not all inventories are the same. What distinguishes one from the other and when can they be performed?

....

....

....

....

....

....

....

....

....

11. What is the spiritual axiom that we face?

....

....

....

12. What might we be victimized by?

....

....

....

13. What do we need in all these situations?

....

....

....

....

....

14. Why do we look for progress not perfection?

....

....

....

....

15. Other than disagreeable or unexpected problems, what other situations call for self-control?

....

....

....

16. What insurance do we have against big-shotism?

....

....

....

17. What is it that we begin to see that leads to true tolerance?

....

....

....

18. When we fail somebody what can we do? What are the keynotes that will help us?

....

....

....

19. What should we do at the end of the day?

....

....

....

20. What odd trait of human emotion permeates human affairs from top to bottom?

....

....

....

Evaluating with Step 10.
To help assess whether you are working a good Step 10, consider the questions below.

Are you continuing to take personal inventory? Outline how you do this.

....

....

....

....

....

....

....

....

....

When you review your day, what sort of things are you including?

....

....

....

....

....

....

....

Do you struggle with admitting when you are wrong?

....

How important is this Step? Why?

....

....

....

....

....

....

....

Whose guidance do you seek before admitting your wrongs?

....

....

....

....

....

Creating with Step 10.
Create new discussion points that may be discussed with a newcomer that will highlight the importance of a continued inventory and the importance of Step 10. Check your points out with a sponsor before talking to a newcomer.

Step 11. "Sought through prayer and meditation to improve our conscious contact with God as we understood Him, praying only for knowledge of His will for us and the power to carry that out."

Remembering Step 11.
You must be able to recall Step 11 from memory before continuing with the next level. Write it down to start with.

....

....

....

....

....

....

....

....

....

....

Understanding Step 11.
To begin the process of understanding this Step take a look at some of the language used. Write a quick definition in your

own words then flip to the back of the book to see the dictionary definitions, how do they compare?

What is your definition of "**sought**"?

....

....

....

We all have an idea of what "**prayer**" means, but what does it mean to you?

....

....

....

Often a word surrounded with myth and false beliefs, what is your understanding of "**meditation**".

....

....

....

....

....

....

....

Write your meaning of the word **"improve"**:

....

....

....

What is your definition of **"conscious"**?

....

....

....

How might you explain "**contact**"?

....

....

....

Try and give your definition of "**God**".

....

....

....

....

....

....

....

....

Again, write down your meaning of "understood".

....

....

....

Next, we shall put those words together in the context of the step.

"Sought through **prayer** and **meditation"**

Talk about prayer with another person; discuss morning and evening prayer and the need for praying on an 'as you need it' basis. Also have a discussion about the point that, to begin with, people are often afraid of meditation. They see it as some mystical experience that only the very spiritually enlightened can do it. Reassure yourself that this is not true and that you will learn more as you progress through this Step. Make some notes on any key points that are made.

....

....

....

....

....

....

....

....

....

"conscious contact".

Talk with your sponsor or another what it means to have **"conscious contact"** with a higher power and the feelings this may bring. How do you know when you are in contact? Make some notes of the discussion.

....

....

....

....

....

"His will for us" Discuss how you know whose will you are following? (You may wish to revisit Step 3 and discuss 'self will run riot'.)

"And the **power** to carry that out". A point for discussion could be that God doesn't do things for us directly but gives us the power, if sought, to do those things ourselves. What do you think? Write your views down.

....

....

....

....

....

....

....

....

....

....

....

....

Applying Step 11.

You must be able to apply the information learned previously in this Step to personal action.

Research different types of meditation techniques, then write a summary of which one best suits your personality i.e. hypnotherapy CD's, soothing music, candles, etc. There are lots of methods out there: Find the one that fits.

....

....

....

....

....

....

....

....

....

....

....

Practice praying. You should start to pray as part of a daily routine.

Analyzing Step 11. (Big Book and 12 and 12 Study Section)
At this level you need to examine A.A.s writings about Step 11. Read the rest of "Into Action" starting at the bottom of page 85 to the end of the chapter. You will also need to read Step 11 in the 12 Steps and 12 Traditions. In order to make the learning process easier during this section, a list of questions has been added below. These will help focus you on specific points in each chapter.

The following questions are based on Into Action in the Big Book Alcoholics Anonymous.

1. What is the Step 11 suggestion?

....

2. What matter should we not be shy on?

....

3.Make a list of what we should look at when we constructively review our day?

....

....

....

....

....

....

....

....

....

....

4. What should you be careful not to drift into?

....

5. What should we do on awakening?

....

....

....

6. What should we ask God to divorce our thinking from?

....

....

7. What should we do when we face indecision?

....

....

....

8. What should we be careful never to pray for?

....

....

9. What should we constantly remind ourselves?

....

....

....

10. Because we are undisciplined, what should we do?

....

....

....

The next questions are concentrating on Step 11 as written in the 12 Steps and 12 Traditions.

11. How are we apt to regard serious meditation and prayer?

....

....

....

12. Despite all the logic and experience, how may newcomers and agnostics view the power of prayer?

....

....

....

13. Why would those of us that have come to make regular use of prayer never do without it?

....

....

....

....

....

14. What happens when we link self-examination, meditation and prayer?

....

....

....

15. How could beginners in meditation start?

....

....

....

....

....

....

....

16. What can you do if troubled by intrusive thoughts?

....

....

....

17. What is self-forgetting?

....

....

....

18. What is prayer described as?

....

....

19.How do you go about it?

....

....

....

....

....

....

....

20. When we have a decision to make, we can pause and say what?

....

....

21. What is hazardous about taking a troubling dilemma straight to God?

....

....

....

....

22. What other temptation can we fall into?

....

....

....

23. What can almost any experienced A.A. tell you?

....

....

....

24. What should you do if seized with a rebellion so sickening that you will not pray?

....

....

....

25. What is one of the greatest rewards of meditation?

....

....

....

Discuss the Serenity Prayer and ask what this prayer means to you.

Evaluating with Step 11.
Assess your position and understanding of Step 11.

Some questions to help with this could be:

What solution could you apply to improving your meditation?

....

....

....

....

....

....

....

When or how often are you praying to your higher power?

....

....

....

How effective do you think this Step is in avoiding relapse?

....

....

....

Why is this Step referred to as a **maintenance** Step?

....

....

....

....

....

Creating with Step 11.

You should now have some ideas that can help implement this Step. Now it is time to put them into action and begin working Step 11 on a daily basis. Make a summary of your plan below.

....

....

....

....

....

....

....

....

....

....

....

....

....

Again, you should create a list of discussion points that may be spoken about with your group, or a newcomer, that will highlight the key points of Step 11.

....

....

....

....

....

....

....

....

....

....

....

....

Step 12. "Having had a spiritual awakening as a result of these steps, we tried to carry this message to alcoholics, and to practice these principles in all our affairs."

Remembering Step 12.
The final step. The last one to learn off by heart. Remember to to do this before proceeding. Start be writing it down.

....

....

....

....

....

....

....

....

....

....

Understanding Step 12.
You must be able to explain the meaning and idea of Step 12. Read the definitions, discuss them and explain them in writing with your own words.

First look at **"spiritual awakening"**. There are different ideas as to what these words mean. Write your understanding below.

....

....

....

....

....

....

What do you think is meant by the word **"message"**.

....

....

....

A definition of **"alcoholic"** could be:

"An alcoholic is someone who has a primary illness or disorder characterised by loss of control over, and addiction to, the drug alcohol. This causes interference in any major life function, e.g. health, family, job, spiritual, friends and legal".

Thats a pretty good definition. However, we know that it just isn't that simple. Alcoholism is often recognized, by those who have it, to be present whether they are drinking or not. Write your interpretation of the word alcoholic.

....

....

....

....

....

....

What are "**principles**"? Makes some notes of your own understanding

....

....

....

What is the meaning of the word "**affairs**" in this context?

....

....

....

Next we shall put each definition into the context of Step 12.

"Having had a spiritual **awakening**"
Talk about what it means to have had a spiritual awakening. Don't worry about going into too much detail as it is covered later.

"As a **result** of these steps"

What is meant by "as a result"? A good discussion point could be "Could I have a spiritual awakening before I complete the Steps"?

"We tried to carry this **message** to **alcoholics**"

Talk about the wording of this part of the Step. Why does it say '**tried**' instead of leaving this word out?

Discuss **which** alcoholics we are trying to carry this message to?

"Practice these **principles** in all our **affairs**".

Discuss the necessity to work this step in every aspect of your life.

Applying Step 12.
You must be able to apply the information learned previously in this Step to your new life. Here are some headings that may help you do this.

Discuss the need to continually practice these principles, remembering that we make mistakes and are only human. Make a few notes on what has been said.

....

....

....

....

....

....

....

Talk through the following statement. "In Step 10 we can promptly admit when our behavior has been wrong but Step 12 is suggesting that we should keep this behavior in check, it should no longer get out of place".

How would you behave in a situation where you felt intimidated or threatened? Why? Write a quick answer.

....

....

....

....

....

....

....

....

What would you say to someone who is still actively drinking?

....

....

....

....

....

....

....

....

....

....

....

Analyzing Step 12. (Big Book and 12 and 12 Study Section)
At this level you will need to examine A.A.s writings about Step 12 and write a breakdown of what the Step means. You will need to read "Working with Others" in the Big Book and Step 12, in the 12 Steps and 12 Traditions.

In order to make the learning process easier during this section, a list of questions has been added below. These will help focus the reader on specific points in each chapter.

The next questions are focusing on Chapter 7, "Working with Others".

1. What has practical experience shown will insure immunity from drinking?

....

....

2. What experience must you not miss?

....

....

....

....

....

3. What should you do when you discover a prospect for A.A.?

....

....

....

4. What might it be wise to do?

....

....

5. When you first meet someone, how should this proceed? List the key points.

....

....

....

....

....

....

....

....

....

....

6. What language had you better use?

....

7. How do we outline the program of action?

....

....

....

8. What should you make clear?

....

....

....

9. If he is not interested in your solution, what may you have to do?

....

....

....

10. How should you proceed if he is sincerely interested?

....

....

....

....

11. What should be your approach if he thinks he can do the job in some other way?

....

....

12. What can you do if your prospect does not respond at once?

....

13. How should your second visit proceed?

....

....

....

14. What is the foundation stone of your recovery?

....

....

....

15. What idea should be burned into the consciousness of every man?

....

....

....

16. How should you deal with divorce or separation?

....

....

....

....

....

17. What can you say to a man who says he cannot recover unless he has his family back?

....

....

....

18. When working with a family what should you take care not to do?

....

19. What can you do assuming you are spiritually fit?

....

....

....

....

....

....

20. What is the rule on not avoiding places?

....

....

....

21. Your job now is to be at the place where what?

....

....

22. What should you be careful never to show?

....

....

....

The following questions are based on Step 12 as written in the 12 and 12.

23. What is the theme of Step 12? What is its key word?

....

....

....

....

....

....

....

24. Each genuine spiritual awakening has something in common. What is it?

....

....

....

....

....

....

....

....

....

25. This chapter asks you to briefly consider what you have been trying to do up to this point and summarizes the Steps so far. Discuss this summary with others and make some bullet points.

....

....

....

....

....

....

....

....

....

....

....

....

....

26. What undreamed rewards can helping another alcoholic bring?

....

....

....

27. What does practically every A.A. member declare?

....

....

....

28. What other kind of 12th Step work is there?

....

....

....

....

....

....

29. How will we come to view setbacks?

....

....

....

30. What is "the biggest question yet"?

....

....

....

31. What is A.A.'s answer to the questions about living?

....

....

32.What are those questions?

....

....

....

....

....

....

....

....

....

....

....

....

....

33. What is it that the best of us can fall for?

....

....

....

34. How do we cope with basic troubles?

....

....

....

35. After we come into A.A. what happens if we keep on growing?

....

....

....

....

....

36. What is the best source of emotional stability?

....

....

37. What will your new inner strength and peace enable you to do?

....

....

38. What special meaning does A.A. have for those of us who were like that?

....

....

39. What has been offset to a surprising extent?

....

....

....

40. What unnatural situations may have developed?

....

....

....

....

....

....

....

41. After long periods of distortion what may be necessary?

....

....

....

42. Why may the wife (a partner) become discontented?

....

....

....

....

43. Separation may be necessary but is often uncommon. What usually happens?

....

....

....

....

44. On the whole what marriages are very good ones?

....

....

45. What is likely to occur when "boy meets girl on A.A. campus"?

....

46. What considerations are equally true and important for those who marry outside of A.A.?

....

....

47. What can be said of members who cannot have a family life?

....

....

....

....

48. What is no longer our principal aim?

....

....

49. What may lead us to become victims of unreasonable fears?

....

....

50. We found out that freedom from fear was more important than what?

....

51. What might 'shipwreck' us during our drinking careers?

....

....

52. What did we find were willing to stay?

....

53. So what did the distinguished men have the nerve to say about us?

....

....

54. What distorted drives have been restored?

....

....

....

....

55. What do we find true leadership depends on?

....

....

56. To get right with ourselves what do we have to do?

....

....

57. Understanding is the key to what?

....

....

58. Action is the key to what?

....

....

59. What do we hope to sense more deeply with each passing day of our lives?

....

....

A spiritual experience is often mistaken for a spiritual awakening. Read and produce a short summary of "A

spiritual experience" (appendix 1 in Alcoholics Anonymous), so as to confirm your understanding of the difference.

....

....

....

....

....

....

....

....

....

....

....

....

....

....

Evaluating with Step 12.

Here you need to assess the importance of Step 12 and consider its significance in your life. Some questions to answer could be;

Do you believe that working these Steps has significantly improved your life? Why?

....

....

....

....

....

....

....

....

Examining your old behavior. How do you think your life would continue if you failed to maintain the new principles you have learned?

....

....

....

....

....

....

....

....

....

How important is it to give it away to keep it? What does this
mean?

....

....

....

....

....

....

....

....

....

What's the implication of a 12 Step call? How do we do it?
What can be the repercussions?

....

....

....

....

....

....

....

Why should it be men with men and women with women?

....

....

....

....

....

....

....

....

What is "two stepping"?

....

....

....

....

....

....

Creating with Step 12.
Here you are to create a list of discussion points that can be talked about with a group or others that helps them to understand the meaning of Step 12. Discuss with a sponsor before leading a group or talking to newcomers.

....

Finally, when having completed the 12 Steps you are to become a sponsor or / and a peer mentor and must apply all this knowledge to educating and nurturing newcomers to the program. Congratulations.

It is by teaching others that we truly understand what we ourselves have been taught.

Space for notes.

Word Definitions.

Admitted
Confess to be true or to be the case, typically with reluctance.
To permit to enter.
Accept as valid.
Allow the possibility of.

Affairs
An event or sequence of events of a specified kind or that has previously been referred to.
A matter that is a particular person's concern or responsibility.

Amends
To correct mistakes made by asking for forgiveness and, or improving the situation that had gone wrong.
Doing what we can to repair the damage that our past behavior has caused.
Something done or given by a person to make up for a loss or injury one has caused.
To change for the better.

Believe
To have confidence or faith in the truth of.
To suppose or assume.
To understand.

Care
Caution in avoiding harm or danger.
Close attention.

Upkeep or maintenance.

Watchful oversight; charge or supervision.

Carry

Take or develop (an idea or activity) to a specified point.

Move someone or something from one place to another.

Have on one's person and take with one wherever one goes.

Character

The mental and moral qualities distinctive to an individual.

The quality of being individual, typically in an interesting or unusual way.

Strength and originality in a person's nature.

A person's good reputation.

Contact

Communicate with typically in order to give or receive specific information.

Touch.

Connect with.

Coming together of two things.

Continued

Remain in existence or operation.

Carry on with.

Keep on working.

To carry on after an interruption.

Persist in an activity or process.

Decision

The act or process of deciding.

Making a judgment.

The act of or need for making up one's mind: This is a difficult decision.

A resolution - He made a good decision.

Defects

A shortcoming or imperfection.

A failing or deficiency.

A mark or flaw that spoils the appearance of something.

Characteristics of an individual that reduce its quality.

Direct

Proceeding without interruption.

Straightforward and candid.

Having no intervening persons i.e. do it yourself.

Consisting of the exact words of the writer or speaker.

Absolute.

Entirely

Wholly or fully.

Completely or unreservedly.

Solely or exclusively.

Without any others being included or involved.

To the full or entire extent.

Exact

Not approximated in any way; precise.

Accurate or correct in all details.

Tending to be accurate and careful about minor details.

Except when

Without the accompanying circumstance.

The task can not be completed unless a condition is met.
Not under any other circumstance.
Unless.

Fearless
Oblivious of dangers or perils.
Calmly resolute in facing fear.
Possessing or displaying courage.
Able to face and deal with danger or fear without flinching.

God
The one Supreme Being, the creator and ruler of the universe.
A supreme being according to some particular conception.
Life, Truth, love.
Mind, Soul, Spirit.
Principle.
Good Orderly Decisions.

Greater
A cut above.
Better.
Higher.
Superior.

Harmed
Physically injure.
Damage the health of.
Have an adverse effect on.
The act of damaging something or someone.

Humble
The quality of being modest.
Never being arrogant.
Marked by meekness or modesty, not arrogant or prideful.

Low in rank, quality, or station.

An admirable quality that not many people possess - means that a person may have accomplished a lot, or be a lot but doesn't feel it is necessary to advertise or brag about it.

To cut one's ego down to size.

Improve

To raise to a more desirable or more excellent quality or condition.

To increase the productivity or value of.

To put to good use; use profitably.

To become better.

To make beneficial additions or changes.

Inventory

A detailed, itemized list, report, or record of things in one's possession.

A periodic survey of all goods and materials in stock.

The process of making such a list, report, or record.

The items listed in such a report or record.

An evaluation or a survey of abilities, assets, or resources.

Injure

Do physical harm or damage to.

Hurt - Harm - Wound – Impair.

To cause distress to.

Wound or injure feelings.

To commit an injustice or offence against.

List

A series of names or other items written or printed together in a meaningful grouping or sequence so as to constitute a record.

To set down together in a list.

Make a list of.
A list does not contain further information.

Lives
All of me.
My behavior and actions.
100% of my time.

Meditation
Contemplation of spiritual matters.
Think intently and at length.
Reflect deeply on a subject.
Training the mind to be calm.
Having one thought at one time.

Message
A verbal, written or recorded communication sent to or left for a recipient who cannot be contacted directly.
A significant point or central theme, especially one that has political, social or moral importance.

Moral
Concerned with or relating to human behavior, especially the distinction between good and bad or right and wrong behavior.
Adhering to conventionally accepted standards of conduct.
Based on a sense of right and wrong according to law.
Having psychological rather than tangible effects.

Nature
The basic or inherent features of something.
The innate or essential qualities or character of a person or animal.

Inborn or hereditary characteristics of personality.
A person of a specified character.

Personal
Of, affecting, or belonging to a particular person rather than to anyone else.
Private.
Individual.
Particular.
Subjective

Power
Force.
Strength.
Authority.
Energy.
A person or organization that is strong or influential within a particular context.

Powerless
Without ability, influence, or power.
Lacking strength.
Being weak and feeble.
Inability to control the use of alcohol or other drugs by self will.
The inability to engage in a behavior moderately.

Prayer
A religious service, esp. a regular one, at which people gather in order to pray together.
A solemn request for help or expression of thanks addressed to God or an object of worship.
An earnest hope or wish .

The act of making a petition to God, a god, or another object of worship.

Principles
A fundamental truth or proposition that serves as the foundation for a system of belief or behavior.
A chain of reasoning.
A rule or belief governing one's personal behavior.
Morally correct behavior and attitudes.

Promptly
Carried out or performed without delay.
At once.
Quick to act as the occasion demands.

Remove
Take something away.
Eliminate or get rid of.
Be distant from.
Be very different from.

Restored
To return to an original or former condition.
To bring back to health, good spirits, etc.
To reintroduce or re-enforce: *to restore discipline.*
To reconstruct (an extinct animal, former landscape, etc.)

Result
A consequence, effect, or outcome of something.
Occur or follow as a consequence.
To come about as an end result.

Sanity

(Psychology) the state of being sane.
Good sense or soundness of judgment.
Free from mental derangement.
Having a sound, healthy mind.

Searching
To go or look through carefully in order to find something missing or lost.
To examine carefully in order to find something concealed.
To explore or examine in order to discover.
To look at or beneath the superficial aspects of, to discover a motive, reaction, feeling or basic truth.

Self-will
A stubborn or obstinate refusal to listen to others.
Pursuing one's own wishes and aims.
The trait of resolutely controlling your own behavior.

Shortcomings
Character defects.
Failure to meet a certain standard.
A fault or defect.
Imperfections that detract from the whole.
The quality or state of being flawed or lacking.

Sought
Attempt to find something.
Attempt or desire to obtain or achieve something.
Ask for something from someone.
Search for and find someone or something.

Spiritual awakening

A spiritual awakening usually involves a realisation that you are no longer the same.

A spiritual awakening involves progressive learning.

A definition in the 12 and 12 says, "the most important meaning of a spiritual awakening is that a person has now become able to do, feel and believe that which he could not do before".

Understood
To perceive the meaning of.

To grasp the significance, implications, or importance of.

To accept as true; believe.

To have knowledge or background, as on a particular subject.

Unmanageable
Difficult or impossible to manage, manipulate, or control.

No longer functions successfully.

Unacceptable consequences of addiction.

A time in life when a person can no longer function successfully by means of the unaided will.

Willing
Of one's own free will.

Freely and spontaneously.

Acting or ready to act gladly; eagerly compliant.

Voluntarily or ungrudgingly.

Wrongs / Wrong
Not correct or true.

Unsuitable or undesirable.

In a bad or abnormal condition; amiss.

Unjust, dishonest, or immoral.

Appendix to Step 6.

Aggressive, belligerent	-	good-natured, gentle
Angry -	-	forgiving, calm, generous
Apathetic	-	interested, concerned, alert
Apprehensive, afraid	-	calm, courageous
Argumentative	-	agreeable
Arrogant, insolent	-	unassuming, humble
Attacking, critical	-	fair, self-restrained
Avoiding	-	faces problems and acts
Blocking	-	honest, intuitive
Boastful	-	modest, humble
Careless	-	careful, concerned
Cheating	-	honest
Competitive (socially)	-	cooperative
Compulsive	-	free
Conceited, self-important	-	humble, modest
Contradictory, oppositional	-	reasonable, agreeable
Contrary, pigheaded	-	reasonable
Controlling	-	lets go, esp. of others lives
Cowardly	-	brave
Critical	-	non-judgmental, tolerant
Cynical	-	open-minded
Deceitful	-	honest
Defensive	-	open to criticism
Defiant, contemptuous	-	respectful
Denying	-	honest, accepting

Dependent	-	accepts help but is self-reliant
Depressed, morose	-	hopeful, optimistic, cheerful
Dirty, poor hygiene	-	clean
Dishonest	-	honest
Disloyal, treacherous	-	faithful, loyal
Disobedient	-	obedient
Disrespectful, insolent	-	respectful, reverent
Enabling	-	boundaries, tough love
Envying	-	empathetic, admiring
Evasive, deceitful	-	candid, straightforward
Exaggerating	-	honest, realistic
Faithless, disloyal	-	reliable, faithful
Falsely modest	-	honest, has self-esteem
Falsely prideful	-	modest, humble
Fantasizing, unrealistic	-	practical, realistic
Fearful	-	confidant, courageous
Forgetful	-	responsible
Gluttonous, excessive	-	moderate
Gossiping	-	close-mouthed, kind, praising
Greedy	-	moderate, generous, sharing
Hateful	-	forgiving, loving, concerned
Hypersensitive	-	tolerant, doesn't personalize
Ill-tempered	-	good-tempered, calm
Impatient	-	patient
Impulsive, reckless actions	-	consistent, considered

Inconsiderate	-	thoughtful, considerate
Indecisive, timid	-	firm, decisive
Indifferent, apathetic, aloof	-	caring
Inflexible, stubborn	-	open-minded, flexible
Insecure, anxious	-	self-confident, secure
Insincere, hypocritical	-	sincere, honest
Intolerant	-	understanding, patient
Irresponsible, reckless	-	responsible
Isolating, solitary	-	sociable, outgoing
Jealous	-	trusting, generous, admiring
Judgmental	-	broadminded, tolerant
Justifying (own actions)	-	honest, frank, candid
Lack of purpose	-	purposeful
Lazy, indolent	-	industrious, conscientious
Loud	-	tasteful, quiet
Lustful	-	healthy sexuality
Lying	-	honest
Manipulative	-	honest, non-controlling
Masked, closed	-	honest, open, candid
Nagging	-	supportive
Narrow minded	-	open minded
Obscene, crude	-	modest, courteous
Over emotional	-	emotionally stable
Perfectionist	-	realistic goals
Pessimistic	-	realistic, hopeful, optimistic

Possessive	-	generous
Prejudiced	-	open-minded
Procrastinates promptly	-	disciplined, acts
Projecting (negative) optimistic	-	clear sighted,
Rationalizing	-	candid, honest
Resentful, bitter, hateful	-	forgiving
Resisting growing	-	willing to grow
Rude, discourteous	-	polite, courteous
Sarcastic	-	praising, tolerant
Self-important	-	humble, modest
Self-centered	-	caring of others
Self-destructive	-	self-fulfilling
Self-hating	-	self-accepting, loving
Self-justifying	-	admitting wrongs, humble
Self-pitying	-	grateful, realistic, accepting
Self-righteous understanding	-	humble,
Self-seeking	-	selfless, concerned for others
Selfish	-	concerned with others
Shy	-	outgoing
Slothful (lazy)	-	industrious, taking actions
Spiteful, malicious	-	forgiving
Stealing	-	honest
Stubborn	-	open-minded, willing
Sullen	-	cheerful
Superior, grandiose	-	humble

Superstitious	-	faithful and trusting
Suspicious	-	trusting
Tense	-	calm, serene
Thinking negatively	-	being positive
Treacherous	-	trustworthy
Undisciplined, self-indulgent	-	disciplined
Unfair	-	fair
Unfriendly, hostile	-	friendly
Ungrateful	-	thankful, grateful
Unkind, mean, spiteful	-	kind
Unsupportive of others	-	supportive
Untrustworthy, unreliable	-	trustworthy
Useless, destructive	-	helpful, constructive
Vain	-	modest, humble
Vindictive	-	forgiving
Violent	-	gentle
Vulgar	-	polite
Wasteful	-	thrifty
Wilful	-	accepting
Withdrawn	-	outgoing
Wordy, verbose	-	frank, to the point, succinct

Bibliography.

Alcoholics Anonymous, 3rd edition. New York: Alcoholics Anonymous World Services Inc, 1976. (The "Big Book.")

Twelve Steps and Twelves Traditions, New York. Alcoholics Anonymous World Services Inc, 1981. (The "Twelve and Twelve")

Concise Oxford English Dictionary. 12th edition. Oxford University Press Oxford, 2011.

Further word definitions from www.thefreedictionary.com

Anderson, L.W. & Krathwohl, D.R. (Eds.) (2001). A taxonomy for Learning, teaching, and assessing: A revision of Bloom's taxonomy of educational objectives. New York: Addison Wesley Longman.

Geoff Petty, Teaching Today, 3rd edition (2004), Nelson Thornes Ltd, Cheltenham, United Kingdom.

Made in the USA
Las Vegas, NV
28 December 2022